EXTREME WEATHER

TSUNAMIS

JACK WILLIAMS

NORWOOD HOUSE PRESS

Cataloging-in-Publication Data

Names: Williams, Jack.
Title: Tsunamis / Jack WIlliams.
Description: Buffalo, NY : Norwood House Press, 2026. | Series: Extreme weather | Includes glossary and index.
Identifiers: ISBN 9781978576926 (pbk.) | ISBN 9781978576933 (library bound) | ISBN 9781978576940 (ebook)
Subjects: LCSH: Tsunamis--Juvenile literature.
Classification: LCC GC221.5 W555 2026 | DDC 551.4673--dc23

Published in 2026 by
Norwood House Press
2544 Clinton Street
Buffalo, NY 14224

Designer: Rhea Magaro
Editor: Kim Thompson

Photo credits: Cover, p1. Gvictoria, Fejas/Shutterstock.com; p. 5 Mimadeo/Shutterstock.com; p. 6 Oskari Porkka/Shutterstock.com; p. 7 Ryan Janssens/Shutterstock.com; p. 8 P Songthongweerakul/Shutterstock.com; p. 9 Tamara Kulikova/Shutterstock.com; p. 10 Mana Photo/Shutterstock.com; p. 12 Adansijav Official/Shutterstock.com; p. 13 FOTOKITA/Shutterstock.com; p. 14 IgorZh/Shutterstock.com; p. 16 Muralonga/Shutterstock.com; p. 18 Andrei Armiagov/Shutterstock.com; p. 19 NOAA.com; p. 20 wisnupriyono/Shutterstock.com

Printed in the United States of America

CPSIA compliance information: Batch #CWNHP26: For further information contact Norwood House Press at 1-800-237-9932.

TABLE OF CONTENTS

WATCH OUT!

Huge ocean **waves** speed toward land.

Watch out! It is a **tsunami** (tsu-NAH-mee).

WHAT IS A TSUNAMI?

A tsunami is a wall of waves that begins deep in the ocean.

The waves race toward **beaches**. They gain strength and speed.

Big changes can happen on the ocean floor. There are underwater **earthquakes**. Underwater **volcanoes** erupt.

Above these events, water rises. It forms powerful waves.

The waves zoom across the ocean faster than a jet plane! They can travel thousands of miles.

Before a tsunami hits land, a strange thing happens. Water on the beach sucks back into the ocean.

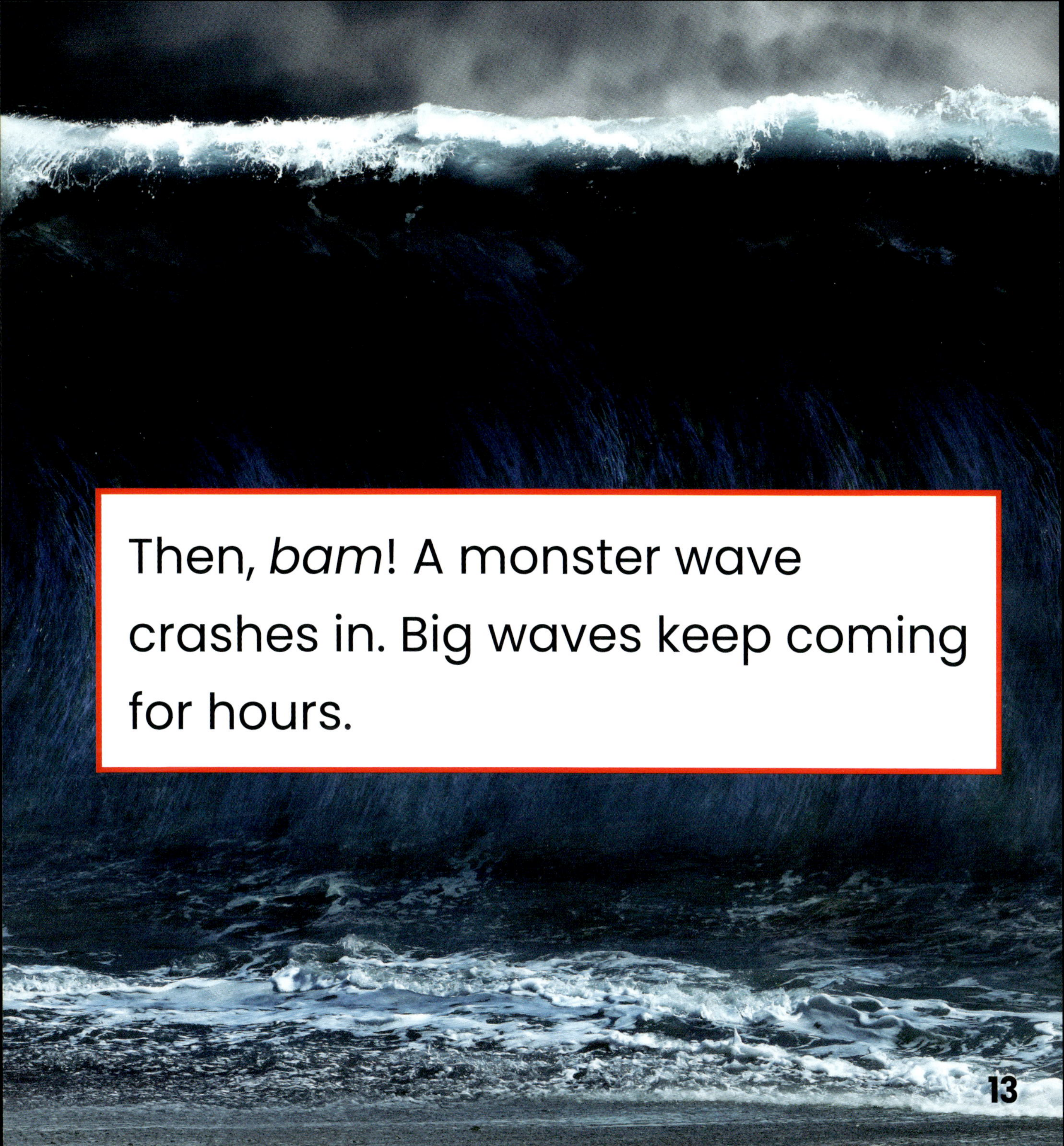

Then, *bam*! A monster wave crashes in. Big waves keep coming for hours.

WHY ARE TSUNAMIS DANGEROUS?

A tsunami wave may be as tall as a 10-story building. It is one of the strongest **forces** in nature.

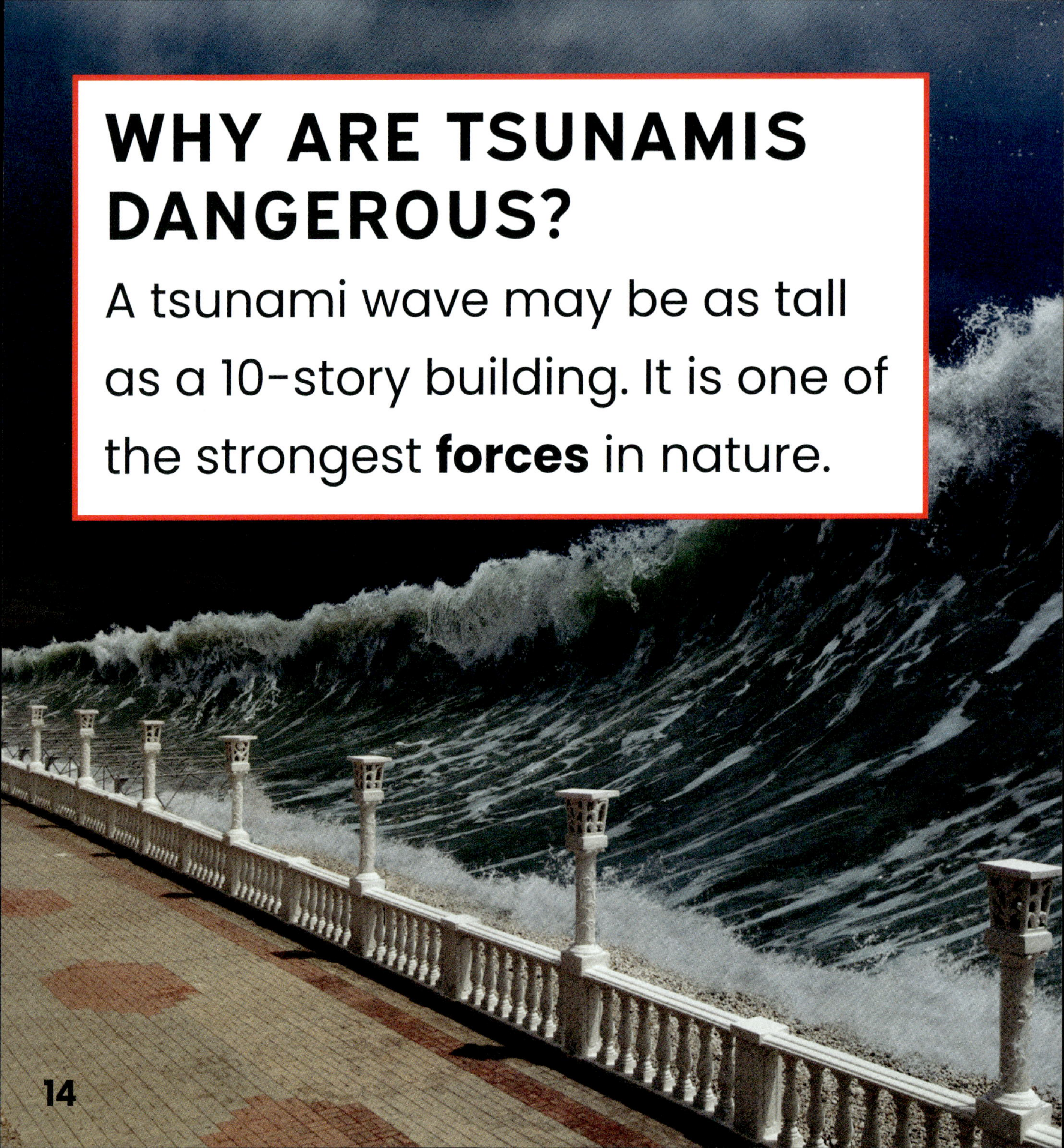

Tsunami waves pick up boats and throw them.

They **uproot** trees.

They **destroy** buildings and whole towns.

HOW TO STAY SAFE

Satellites watch the ocean. They **detect** waves that may become tsunamis. Scientists warn people.

TSUNAMI
NOAA
S220

TSUNAMI
EVACUATION
ROUTE

If a tsunami is on the way, do not wait.

Run to high ground. Stay far away from beaches.

GLOSSARY

beaches (BEE-chis): strips of sand or gravel at the edge of the ocean or another body of water

destroy (dih-STROY): to break something completely so it cannot be used anymore

detect (di-TEKT): to discover something or become aware of it

earthquakes (URTH-kwayks): times when Earth's tectonic plates move against each other and cause sudden, violent shaking of the ground

forces (FOR-siz): strong powers that can push, pull, or move things

satellites (SAT-uh-lites): spacecrafts sent into orbit around a planet

tsunami (tsu-NAH-mee): a series of large, destructive ocean waves usually caused by underwater earthquakes

uproot (up-ROOT): to pull a plant completely out of the ground so its roots can be seen

volcanoes (vahl-KAY-nohs): mountains with openings through which lava, ash, and hot gases erupt

waves (wayvz): lines of water that rise up and move across the surface of the ocean

THINKING QUESTIONS

1. What can cause a tsunami?
2. What happens right before a tsunami hits land?
3. How tall can tsunami waves be?
4. What can tsunamis destroy?
5. How do scientists know a tsunami is coming?

INDEX

ABOUT THE AUTHOR

Jack Williams is curious about all things in nature, especially the weather! He checks the weather forecast every day. He used to be a police officer, so he knows how important it is to watch out for danger and stay safe.